THE REPUBLICAN PARTY IN TENNESSEE REORGANIZED.

TO THE

REPUBLICANS OF TENNESSEE

AND THE

UNITED STATES.

Memorial, Resolutions and Proceedings had at a Convention held at the Capitol,

NASHVILLE, FEBRUARY 16TH, 1870,

TOGETHER WITH THE SPEECHES OF

HONS. A. J. FLETCHER AND J. O. SHACKELFORD.

The Finance Committee, to whom was assigned the task of preparing for publication the proceedings of the Convention, take pleasure in placing before the Republicans of the country the following record of business transacted, which they hope will do much to give confidence, insure active co-operation and place the Republican army of Tennessee in condition to make a bold and successful resistance to the rapid and unblushing efforts of a rebel Democracy to strike down all that remains to protect those who loved and dared help maintain the Union when it was in danger. We ask the Union men of Tennessee to read this paper, circulate it and prepare to organize in every county to defeat the nefarious schemes of a horde of States Rights Democrats. Let us prepare to protect the lives and property of all our fellow-citizens without regard to condition, race or color.

"Let us have peace."

THE COMMITTEE.

PROCEEDINGS

OF THE

CONVENTION.

On Wednesday, Feb. 16, a Convention of Delegates from all parts of the State, assembled at the Capitol to organize and perfect a plan to put the Republicans of this State in condition to make some resistance to the overwhelming tide of modern Rebel Democracy that is subverting all that is left of Republicanism in the Constitution and laws of the State.

At twelve o'clock the Hall of the House of Representatives was filled with eager expectant Republicans; Hon. A. J. Fletcher called the meeting to order and nominated Hon. D. A. Nunn as permanent Chairman, which was unanimously carried. Secretaries were appointed and the Convention proceeded to business.

On motion the following were appointed a Committee on Resolutions: A. J. Fletcher, J. H. Agee, A. Smith and J. M. Tommeny.

While the committee were preparing their resolutions, the Hon. H. H. Harrison was called upon for re marks, who responded in a speech full of patriotic, hopeful sentiments.

The Committee upon Resolutions reported the following:

Resolved, That we indorse and approve of the platform of principles adopted by the Republican National Convention at Chicago in May, 1868, and that we deem a further declaration of principles unnecessary at the present time.

Resolved, That we hereby earnestly invite all persons in the State, well disposed to the National Government, irrespective of former party affiliations, to unite with us in rescuing the State from the domination of a corrupt, proscriptive and oppressive Democratic party.

Resolved, That notwithstanding our isolated and oppressed condition, we have an abiding confidence that the General Government will extend to us that protection which is due to true and tried allegiance and which we so greatly need.

Resolved, That we approve of the fourteenth and fifteenth amendments to the Constitution of the United States, and that the safety of the loyal people of Tennessee urgently demands the enforcement of said fourteenth amendment by appropriate and speedy legislation by Congress.

Resolved, That we regard the so-called Constitutional Convention, now in session in this city, as irregular and revolutionary, and that we disapprove and condemn its entire proceedings; especially their proposition to strike down the present judiciary of the State, and to annex a condition to the right of the poor man to vote.

Resolved, That we approve of the course of the Republican members of the present Legislature; while we regard much of the action of the majority of said body as partsian and oppressive in the extreme, and we denounce as violative of the right of free speech and freedom of the press the proceedings now going on against those who signed the call for this meeting.

which were unanimously carried.

D. W. Peabody, of Davidson, moved that a State Central Committee of sixteen, two from each Congressional District, be appointed by the Chairman, and that he report the names at the mass meeting to be held at the Court House to-night. Carried.

Col. Beaumont moved that a Committee of five be appointed to collect facts of outrages upon Republicans in the State, and that they report to the State Central Committee. Carried.

The Chairman named the following gentlemen as that Committee: A. J. Fletcher, T. A. Kerchival, T. R. Tannett, S. B. Beaumont and A. A. Carter.

The Chair announced that a business meeting of delegates would be held at the Stacey House at 3 o'clock P. M.

The Convention having completed

its business, adjourned to meet in the Court House at 7½ P. M.

AT THE COURT HOUSE.

A large concourse of Republicans assembled at the Court House in the evening, and after organization the members of the State Central Committee were announced as follows:

STATE CENTRAL COMMITTEE.

1st District—A. H. Pettibone, A. W. Howard,

2d District—M. L. McConnell, John C. Tate.

3d District—Thos. Waters, R. S. Kindrick.

4th District—W. H. Wisener, W. T. Elliott.

5th District—Jno. Trimble, Jno. J. Carey, Nashville.

6th District—G. W. Blackburn, Fielding Hurst.

7th District—W. W. Murray, A. E. Boone.

8th District—J. L. Poston, W. T. Kennedy,

Who will meet at Nashville Thursday, February 24th, for organization and business.

The following memorial and resolution from the colored men were read and adopted:

TO THE PRESIDENT:

We, the loyal people of this State, in mass meeting assembled, to take in consideration the outrages committed upon us, and to devise some means to relieve, as far as possible, the loyal people from their unfortunate position, by being the prey of a well organized band of outlaws, pro wling about the State, committing depredations that would set to blush the darkest ages of the world; crimes the most heinous committed under the cover of night, and by day, with impunity. We have suffered long, and lost many of our best men both white and colored, and notwithstanding that, we had heped that the time had come when we would not have to make an appeal to you, for the protection of our lives and property; but to our discomfort and the displeasure of every good citizen living in our State, crime is largely on the increase of the nature discribed above. We have appealed in vain to the authoriys of our State, and in every instance it has only proved more injurious to our people, so much so that it is with great difficulty that the colored people can be induced to give information of their true condition. Having thus exhausted every means known to us legally, to seek redress or check the outrages perpetrated upon the colored people, as a last resort, and the highest known to our country, we now appeal to you, sir, to give us some relief. We find that since the authorities of our State are indifferent to our appeals, either from an intimacy with many of these outlaws, or from fear of their powerful organization, to even make an attempt to feret out the guilty, and bring to justice and punish those that should be the last to escape, sir! we appeal to you, in the name of justice, in the name of the hard working men of our State, in the name of our wives and children, and in the name of our country and her honor, to send us some relief. We have invited the envy of these people by our devotion to this Government, and can it be possible that our Government intends to give us over again to the tender mercies of these people. The war in open combat where soldiers decided the disputes of their country, has ceased, they have merely returned from the field to the farms and cities, in ten thousand forms upon the labor and loyal people of the State, seeking revenge for past defeat; we therefore, pray that you will, by special message to the Congress of the United States, make known our condition here, or by some means best suited to your judgment, send us some relief. The people are being taken from their beds at night or from prisons and hanged or shot down like beasts, and it would seem as though they were taken and put in prison for the convenience of these lawless bands.

Hear this, our first appeal, and we hope it may be the last of its kind, is the prayer of the ill-used and loyal people of our State, and we will ever pray for you and our country.

Resolved, That this memorial be sent to our Representatives in Congress with the request that they be presented to the President of the United States.

After which speeches were made by the Hon. A. J. Fletcher and Hon. J. O. Shackelford.

SPEECH OF HON. A. J. FLETCHER'

At an adjourned meeting, at the Court House, at night, the Hon. A. J. Fletcher addressed the assembly.

He said: That his relation to the present meeting was certainly interesting. In the first place, any speaker, addressing a Republican audience in Tennessee, at this crisis, speaks, as it were, with a halter around his neck, and with a consciousness, that the muzzle of a pistol may be at his brain in a few hours. But he, (the speaker) incurred the additional hazzard of impeachment, censure and arrest by the Legislature and the so-called Constitutional Convention, now in session. As Secretary of State of Tennessee, these bodies had him completely in their power. They might depose him, they might impeach him, they might censure him, and they might libel him on their journals, as he believed they would, and he had no redress. The Kuklux or Pale Faces, might hang him as they had Barmore, or shoot him as they had Senator Case and a thousand others, but the Constitution of Tennesssee guaranteed to him the freedom of speech, and of the press and the right to speak his mind on political questions, and he proposed to do so, so long as that Constitution was in force, and so long as we had the form of free government. Be the consequence to myself what they may (said the speaker) whether it be deposition, impeachment, censure, or the halter, I intend to arraign the present Legislature and Convention and the party in power in Tennessee for usurpation, disloyalty and oppression. The loss of an office or even of one life was a small matter in comparison with the great rights now endangered and, it may be, lost.

What, sirs, have we witnessed in this city in the last few days? Half a dozen gentleman meet by accident. They are Republicans. They talk over the condition of things in the State. They know that the words and actions of Republicans are daily misrepresented and tortured by the press. They see a vast secret organization first known as "Kuklux" and then "Pale Faces," nightly riding over the country in masks and shrouds, butchering, in cold blood, at the hour of midnight, the unoffending citizens, and such acts either suppressed or grossly misrepresented and directly or indirectly justified. They see a Legislature in session repealing every law on the statute book that may afford any protection to the loyal citizens, and enacting just such laws as they can or dare enact for their oppression. They see a Convention, calling itself a Constitutional Convention, assembled without authority of law, laying its hands upon the most sacred rights guaranteed to the citizen. They see, in short, that the government of law has ceased and that brute force, armed and masked, governs the State. One gentleman, an old and honored native of the State, suggests that a newspaper ought to be started with the courage to lay these things before the country, and another suggests the importance of organizing the Republicans of this State into a party on great national principles, and they separate with an agreement to see other friends and invite them to unite in an effort to effect these results. Finally they agree to send out a circular letter, calling attention to these facts and these necessities, and inviting Republicans to meet at the Capital of the State to confer together on the subject of their common welfare. The circular letter was written and signed by eighteen citizens, printed and sent by mail to prominent Republican in different parts of the State. It is written, it is true, in plain and direct language, but no stronger than was usual with the Whigs and Democrats in similar proceedings in former days. It states, in brief, that the crisis is alarming, that violence prevails in many parts of the State, and that the acts of the Legislature and Convention are oppressive. Its design was to call an ordinary political meeting for ordinary and practical purposes, but it is true at an extraordinary crisis. No sooner was the circular made public than the attention of the Legislature was called to it. Not, it is true, by a member of any experience or weight of character, but, as might be expected, by the busiest, most meddlesome and most officious of them all. Yet, sirs, proceedings were commenced in the Legislature against those who proposed to call the meeting and was voted for by the party in power almost unanimously. A committee with power to send for persons and papers was raised and it was declared in the debate and in the newspapers that the Sergant-at-arms should bring these parties before the committee and that they be put upon their oath as to their designs. The proposed meeting was denounced as a conspiracy and state officials who had signed the call were promised impeachment and deposition. The com mittee met in hot haste, and, without a particle of evidence, a proposition was made and seriously considered for the expulsion of the twelve Republican members who had signed the circular. But it was thought best, though this expulsion was then apparently a foregone conclusion, to go through with some form of trial. It was determined at one time to put these eighteen persons UNDER THE RULE, and send for them one at a time and examine them secretly. But this Lilliputian Star-chamber backed down from this and concluded only to send the Sergeant-at-arms for them, one at a time. They selected for their first victim a member of the House that they thought they could most easily embarrass and intimidate. The Sergeant-at arms took him before the committee. He begged them for counsel. He implored them for permission to send for witnesses to prove himself guiltless of offence. But, sirs, this august and majestic committee were deaf to all these supplications. They parried his applications and excused themselves upon the false and hypocritical ground that he was not on trial, but that he had arraigned the Legislature and that they were trying that august body. It was in vain that this plain and modest farmer refered to the Bill of Rights and to the liberty of speech and of the press. They were inexorable and demanded of him what right he had to make the charges against the Legislature of Tennessee.

But I will say no more now of these proceedings as I expect to be taken before this committee myself. Yet, I will say a word as to the persons who signed the call for this "conspiracy." Of myself I wish to say but little. I am known as a liberal or conservative Republican. I was one of the first to advocate the removal of all disabilities from those who had taken part in the rebellion. But I did not think it necessarily followed that I had to join the rebel Democratic party.

I believed in the great progressive ideas of the national Republican party, and thought I had the right to act with it. I could not join the Democratic party because I did not imbibe its principles and because I could not act with any party that resorted to intimidation and secret murder by masked mobs as a part of its party machinery–that carried elections by such horrible appliances. I had no mask or shroud—no wedding garments for the horrid nuptials

The next name that appears to the call is that of the Hon. J. O. Shackelford who has for years occupied a seat on the Supreme Court Bench and who rendered that decision which restored thirty or forty thousand rebels to the elective franchise. I remember to have seen him a year ago, present in person, a numerously signed petition to the Legislature, asking for the repeal of the franchise law. Next comes the name of the Hon. John Trimble, of Nashville, one of your old and most honored citizens, and who has at all times, and under all circumstances, advocated universal suffrage and universal amnesty. Then there is ex-Senator Elliott, known as a liberal Republican, and who, in his place as Senator, one and two years ago, advocated the most liberal policy.

Col. G. W. Blackburn, State Comptroller, also a man of moderate and liberal ideas and of spotless reputation for integrity. Next appears the name of Col. Peabody, Collector of Internal Revenue, a gentleman of harmless life and liberal ideas. Then follows the names of the twelve Republican members of the Legislature—plain, honest men, from the mountains — conscientious Union men, whose greatest sin, in the estimation of a majority of the Democrats, was committed in defeating Andrew Johnson for United States Senator..

Such are the "conspirators" who have dared to call this meeting, and who are to be called to account through an arresting officer, for calling in question the acts of the Legislature.

I propose to enumerate and to review a portion of the acts of this Legislature, and to show that they are oppressive to the white and colored Unionists of the State, and that they will have, and were intended to have this effect.

I pass over the organization of the Legislature and take no exception to their defeating a gallant Union officer for Clerk of the House, and their election of ex-Confederates to nearly all the offices in their gift. Offices amount to nothing unless the officer has power to oppress. I pass to the laws they have enacted, or propose to enact.

There is quite a prevalent idea that under that provision of the constitution, all laws are to be equal and uniform throuhout the State, no law can be passed that will not oppress one class as much as another. I confess that at one time I greatly relied upon this idea. But I was mistaken. This Legislature have taught me that when there is a *will* there is a *way*. Those who will carefully examine the proceedings of the Legislature will be struck with the adroitness and ingenuity with which they have cheated the constitution in this respect.

They repealed the common school law. I know they pretend to plead high taxes and an embarrassed treasury, in justification of this act; but I, who have been here, on the ground, happen to know their purposes and motives in doing so. The people had not complained of the school tax. On the contrary they have paid it with pleasure. I am aware that members point to certain defects in the machinery of the law as pretexts for its total repeal. But these defects might have been easily corrected by amendment. I happen to know their real motives for this repeal.

1. This common school law was the only hope of the colored children of the State. Legislators hated the freedmen, and therefore went for the repeal of the school tax. They argued that the negroes had but little property, and paid but little taxes, and yet would get an equal share of the benefits. An argument that is at war with free schools under any circumstances.

2. It was a property tax, and it so happened that East Tennessee had, proportionally, the least amount of property and the greatest number of children. Among the high mountains, pure atmosphere, and crystal waters of East Tennessee we are most successful in raising children. But the fathers of these children had committed the sin of loyalty. They had gone into the Federal army, and for that reason the school tax was cut off. With this Legislature loyalty is the original sin, and they have visited the sins of the fathers upon the children. Yes, gentlemen, if it should ever be your fortune to ride through the hills and valleys of East Tennessee, and to see the little white headed boys and girls sporting among the flowers of her hillsides, or gamboling in the shadows of her great mountains, you may say to them, "*but for the loyalty of your fathers you would be at school learning to read the scriptures.*" The repeal of the school law was a rebel blow, most effectually dealt. It struck a loyal and hated race, and a loyal and hated section. But let us look to other laws.

When the Legislature met they found a law upon the statute book "to preserve the public peace." It was a law of a stringent character against masked murderers. It not only proposed to punish them, but it disabled them from sitting upon juries. To use a cant phrase, the Legislature "went for" this law. They repealed it in hot haste! And what was the consequence? In less than ten days gentlemen — chivalrous Southern gentlemen—were riding at night in masks and shrouds, armed as brigands, whipping, shooting and hanging the helpless colored man and the unprotected white loyalist, and dropping notices at the gates of citizens, from the Grand Cyclops, commanding them to leave the State. It was only last Saturday night that I passed from Chattanooga to this city against the warning advice of friends, and heard the thrilling whistle of the Kuklux at three different points on the road, and saw them in ghastly costume around the train. On reaching what I supposed to be a place of safety, a train of thought came into my mind. My early ideas of Southern chivalry! The great Washington was a Southern chivalier! Marion and Horry and Jasper were representatives of the chivalry of 1776, and so were Jefferson and Madison and the Lees and Carrols and Haynes. At a later day was Jackson and Coffee and Carroll, of Tennessee. These were the representatives of the chivalry of their day. They despised a mean action. Their instincts were all noble; and though they may have thought too much of what is called the code of honor, they felt bound to protect the weak and defenceless. Certainly they despised cowardice and cruelty. Yet, here we have the chivalry of 1870!! closely masked, armed as brigands, we see them at the midnight hour, hovering around a railroad train seeking the life of some passenger whose only offense is that he is a Republican, or we hear of them in some lonely cabin butchering the inmates in cold blood because their skin is black and they dare to live. The latest type of Southern chivalry! Great God! How hath the mighty fallen! What degeneration and demoralization!

Next comes another law which, like all the others, has a modest and innocent caption. It is entitled "an act to amend the criminal laws of this State." It simply provides that no person shall vote out of the district or ward in which he resides, and annexes a severe penalty to its violation. The Constitution only requires that a voter shall be a citizen *of the county* in which he offers to vote; but this act requires that he shall be a citizen of the district. Such a law was never thought of before, and, of course, there must be some matters *in pais* to explain this enactment. I will tell you. The chivalry have always boasted that they could control the colored vote. They say to the colored voter before election day that they will stop his wages if he votes the Republican ticket. The landholder tells him he will turn him out of house and home if he does so. If this is not sufficient, a notice from the Grand Cyclops, is left at his door, at night, to the effect that he will be killed if he votes the Republican ticket. To escape those dangers, the colored man has been in a habit of going to the town or some other district, where he might cast his vote in peace—unmolested. Sometimes he found at the county towns a company of militia or regular soldiers, with orders to protect him. This law was passed to compel the colored voter to go to the polls under the eye of his employer or landlord—a temporary master. The law is unconstitutional and has been admitted to be so by the Convention now in session, who have provided for it by conferring the power on the Legislature to pass such laws hereafter.

Then there was the law passed by a former Legislature to prohibit common carriers, railroads, steamboats &c., from making unjust discrimination among passengers on account of race or eolor. Briefly it provided that when a colored man paid his money and bought him a first-class ticket he should have as good accommodation as a white man. This law was repealed without ceremony, so that now the eolered man may be stowed away in the hold of a boat or in a cattle car with his ffrst-class ticket in his pocket.

I next come to the repeal of A CLASS of laws that had been enacted for the protection of loyal men. Several laws existed authorizing the Governor to arm and equip State Guards and especially to protect voters from violence on election days. There was also a law giving to sheriffs, in case of necessity, a permanent *posse* of twenty-five men to assist him in making arrests and executing process. There was also a law authorizing discharged Union soldiers to carry arms for self defence. Every one of thes laws have been swept from the statute book. They had elected the present Governor. His name was at the head of their ticket, but they knew him to be a Union man and that he would have a conscientious desire to execute the laws. They, therfore, disarm him of all power and unmistakably betray their intention to protect their Kuklux or Pale Face allies. It is true this singularly hypocritical body have since gone through with *the form* of passing some sort of a law against masked marauders; *but this is in a horn.*

No person expects any one to be convicted under that law. It does not make Kuklux ineligible as jurors or disqualify them from holding office, As an evidence that the passage of this pretended-law was mere childs play, the fact is so that at the very time the bill was pending they were passing a law incorporating the Pale Faces,(which is only a new name for Kuklux,) and by resolution tendered the use of the Representative Hall to a meeting of the order. And they actually held a banquet and ball in the Capitol, largely attended by this invitation of the Legislature.

There has never been, for all the outrages that have been committed in this State by men in mask A SINGLE INSTANCE of PUNISHMENT.

Again, when this Legislature Assembled they found nearly all the offices in the State filled by loyal Republicans. They had no power to remove them, but like Haman by Mordecai, they could have no peace so long as these Republicans were in office.

It is no plea for them that many of these officers, like myself, cared but little for the offices they held. The principle is the same. Three Supreme Judges, eighteen Circuit Judges, twelve Chancellors, and some twenty Attorneys General, with about three thousand Justices of the Peace, and three hundred county officers had as good a legal title to their offices as they had to their farms or their horses. But to use the same cant phrase I used a moment ago; the Legislature must "go for them." They could not impeach or depose these judges and county officers by law. Still they had to be destroyed, and to effect this they resorted to the extraordinary and revolutionary expedient of calling a sovereign convention. They had no constitutional power to call this convention. They admit they had none. And there was no necessity for such convention. They scarcely pretend that there was. The pretext for a convention was the abrogation of the franchise law. Every one knows that the decisions of the Supreme Court and the registration of last summer had rendered the franchise law a dead letter. This was no part of the object of calling a convention. It was to turn all the loyal men in the State out of office, and to fill the offices with the friends of the lost cause.

Does any one believe that if Judge Hawkins, of the Supreme Court, had lost an arm in the service of the "lost cause"—that if McClain had lost a leg—if Andrews had his honorable scars; and if the Circuit Judges and Chancellors all had honorable discharges from the Confederate service, that any convention would have been called, or that their offices would have been vacated? Those who are posted understand exactly this whole subject. Never, since deliberative bodies met, has there been a greater *sham* than this so-called Constitutional Convention. It is a pretense. It met ostensibly to amend the constitution, but the constitution needed no amendment. Everybody was satisfied with it as it was. Still, they had to go through with the motion. They met and took up every part of the constitution, one after another. Their committees pretended to recommend many radical changes, but they never intended to make any material change except to vacate the offices of the State. They recommended, they altered, they amended, but took care in the end, to leave the constitution about as they found it, but they never lost sight of the offices—especially the judiciary. That is what they came for and that they determined to have. Whatever title may be bestowed by the historian on the National Convention of 1776 or our State Conventions of 1796 and 1834, this convention sitting in the good year of 1870 must, if truthfully named, be called *the Office Hunters' Convention*.

Is there no oppression in this? The lawyer has closed his office to accept a seat on the bench, the farmer or mechanic has been elected to a county office, and has changed his business and made his arrangements for a term of years in office. This convention turns him out remorselessly, and in some cases ruins him, and all for political purposes. And what a precedent is here established! If the Republicans triumph next year they may call a convention and vacate the offices! [A voice: "Will the Republicans ever carry the State?] I am asked from the crowd if this is possible. I answer: not so long as the Democratic party can send out men in mask to intimidate voters on the eve of elections by threats of death, and keep them from the polls or compel them to vote as they desire. The Republicans cannot use Kuklux and Pale Faces in politics. It is contrary to their principles. And if it were otherwise, it is not likely they could command the services of this latest type of Southern chivalry.

If the loss of offices were all, it would be a trifle—nothing. But far more serious troubles await us. I have information from various sources to the effect that thousands of suits are already cut and dried for Union officers and soldiers for acts during the war in the discharge of their duty to the government. For the obedience to orders in the impressment of supplies and the occupation of lands, these gallant men are to be impoverished as soon as a congenial judiciary can be had for the purpose. And this is an ulterior object of this convention.

The Legislature also found another law on the statute book. It was entitled "An act to secure to loyal citizens of Tennessee, recompense from the United States for losses incurred during the rebellion." The great object of this law was to take and perpetuate testimony to establish losses sustained during the war. The papers were to be forwarded to the General Government by the Governor. The Legislature "went for it" and the law was repealed. Not because it was any longer any considerable expense to the State. That had been already incurred and and paid. But it was a law for the benefit and relief of Union men, and that was enough to insure its repeal by the Legislature. *Now*, the Governor has no authority to present these claims. And it was with some hesitancy they allowed these claimants to call for their papers and get them into their own possession. Then, there was the law "to encourage immigration to this State." It appropriated the pittance of $1,000 per annum, the object of which was to advertise the resources and advantages of this State to immigrants. It was repealed, I presume, upon the ground, stated by some, that we wanted no d—d Yankees in Tennessee.

And why, sirs, was not the public debt provided for? Why did the Legislature deliberately reduce the revenues and put it out of their power to pay the interest on the State debt? Had the people complained of high taxes? Not the loyal people, I am sure. Nor had others complained more than was usual when taxation was merely nominal. But, sirs, the argument was openly made that our bonds were held by *Northern men*—that northern men had set our negroes free to the value of four billions, and had devastated our country to the amount of four billions more in damages during the war, and that we should make a set-off of the forty millions we owed them. This idea appears to be the basis of our financial programme. Many of the propositions on financial matters look unmistakably to repudiation. I have not time here to review these financial measures. On a different occasion I may do so. But I will state now that I regard the State as having repudiated, so far as this Legislature has the power to repudiate.

The General Government donated 300,000 acres of land to establish an Agricultural College in this State. After a long debate and the most careful consideration, this college was located at Knoxville, a high and healthy location. The act locating it was in the nature of a contract. The University was to purchase a farm, provide Professors, and enter into bond in the sum of $800,000 for the faithful preservation of the fund, with all of which they have strictly complied and had actually received the greater part of the fund; the contract was, in fact, executed. Yet, sirs, when the present Legislature met they had no thought of letting the college remain at such a hot bed of Unionism as Knoxville. A committee was appointed to investigate, etc. The facts were so patent they were compelled at first to report truthfully. But this did not satisfy the political animus of this august body. They reconsidered and met again, and I understand are determined to take the college away from East Tennessee—that hated section—whose great crime is that 30,000 of her sons went to the field and stood by the flag of their country during the war.

And here a long series of oppressive laws occur to me, but they are not of a general character like those I have named; still it is more tyrannical for a Legislature to direct its blows at individuals than against a class, or rather I should say such legislation is an evidence of a worse spirit.

Why was the Metropolitan Police law repealed? All admit it to have been an excellent system. Most of the principal cities of America have tried and approved it. It had restored order and kept down crime in the Capital of the State. But unfortunately the Commissioners and officers of the police were Union men. This was enough. and in haste the law was repealed. Why was the first Criminal Cricuit Court abolished? Because the Judge was an outspoken Union man.

Why was the seventeenth Circuit abolished? Because the Judge of that Circuit had been a Federal Colonel and was known to be a bold, outspoken Union man.

Why were the laws creating county judgships in eight or ten counties repealed? Because the County Judges in nearly all of these counties were Union men. The case of Judge Leonard of Memphis, occurs to me as illustrative of the animus of this Legislature. That gentleman had held the office of County Judge of Shelby county since 1865. His integrity was impeachable. His reputation was spotless. Yet, sirs, his office was abolished, simply, as was publicly declared at the time, "to get clear of a d—d Radical." But, sirs, the necessity of the office was such that they turn round immediately and propose a bill to re-enact the office, only under a little different name.

Then there were the different boards of County Commissioners throughout the State. Time had demonstrated the necessity of an executive board for the management of county affairs, and experience had proven the wisdom of the system. But, sirs, nearly all these commissioners were Union men, and this was enough for this Legislature to know. They were swept away—annihilated.

Then there are other measures which have been matured and approved and which I presume will pass. I will allude to one or two of these, briefly They have matured and passed, I believe, through one branch a bill under the innocent title of "An act to amend the criminal laws of this State." And what is it? It declares it a crime to hunt in the woods of another, to fish in the waters of another or to pass over the lands of another *without permission.* At first reading the object and design of the bill does not at once appear, but when its practical operation is looked to, it will be understood. Heretofore the passing over the lands of another has been a technical or constructive tresspass, not practically punishable. It was technically only a civil injury, and the damages only nominal and recoverable at heavy cost. This proposed act makes it a high crime, punishable by heavy fine and imprisonment. Now what is the object of this proposed law? The colored man has no land. He has just emerged from a state of slavery, and has had no time to acquire real estate. The great body of the real estate of Tennessee, belongs to ex-Confederates. The practical operation of this law will be that the land owner will permit all good Southern men to fish in his creek, hunt in his woods or pass over his lands, but he will proclaim that negroes and Lincolnites will be indicted for doing so. At any rate, no good Southern man will ever be prosecuted for this crime, while the colored man will find himself in jail for treading down a blade of grass or catching a minnow in the nearest creek.

Then there is a bill pending which prohibits a renter from selling less than a bale of cotton without the consent of the land owner on which the cotton was grown. The object of this bill is palpable. The land owner may, *and will*, refuse his permission to the poor negro to sell his little crop of cotton and will take it at his own price, or nothing. It amounts to a proposition to give the landlord power *to confiscate* the labor of the poor colored man. If this bill does not pass, it will be voted down for fear of offending the sentiment of the majority of the nation. I might stand here till the gray dawn of morning enumerating and explaining the oppressive acts of this Legislature, but time forbids and I must pass on.

I have not commented upon the proposition of the convention to annex to the right of suffrage the condition of the payment of a poll tax. I have but a moment to devote to it. Whatever may be the merits of this proposition, the party in power in this State are estopped from advocating this doctrine. For four years past they have contended that suffrage was a personal right—a natural, inalienable right—and that no power could deprive a citizen of it. They have clamored themselves hoarse in favor of this doctrine. Yet, sirs, when it suits their convenience they qualify the right of suffrage! What is the object of this restriction upon suffrage? They intend, sirs, by indirection and by the power of wealth and management to render the condition of the negro as miserable as possible—to work him through the summer and fall and then—as some planters do mules—to turn him out at winter to starve. Hundreds are now leaving the State on account of that kind of treatment. There can be no question that this suffrage qualification is a blow aimed at the negro.

When the distinguished gentleman who preceded me alluded to the school fund, I heard cheers among those on the back seats. I have thus discovered that there are some Pale Faces or Kuklux present. Though I had not intended to do so, I propose right here to take up this subject of the school fund of Tennessee. I happen to understand this subject, and I will show you what has become of the school fund of Tennessee.

For more than a year past the rebel press of Tennessee have abounded in cries of "school fund thieves," "Radical robbers of the school fund," "robbers of the poor children," etc., and it is stated that the school fund of Tennessee was by Radical manipulation converted into prey for the loyal brotherhood."

There is not, as I will proceed to show, one syllable of truth in, nor the slightest foundation for, any of these charges. On the contrary, every dollar of the school fund of Tennessee was appropriated by the rebel leaders of Tennessee between the 15th of March, 1862 and the 15th of May, 1865. It was carried away at the former date by order or permission of the Confederate Legislature of 1861-2. It consisted of a little over two and a half million dollars and not one cent of this vast sum was ever returned to Tennessee. Not one dollar of the school fund of Tennessee ever went into the hands or became subject to the control of any Republican Legislature or of any Republican official. No! when the dark storm cloud of civil war was lifted from the State, its sacred school fund was gone--gone like the dew of the morning before the rising sun. Every dollar of it had been paid out *in support of treason*, in aid of what is now so mournfully denominated "*the lost cause*." The only showing the custodians of "the school fund of Tennessee" had when they returned to the State was the exact amount of the sacred fund in the shape of Confederate bonds! This is precisely what became of "the school fund of Tennessee" and it now lies among the wreck of the Bank of Tennessee payable "six months after the ratification of a treaty of peace between the Confederate government and the United States!"

A very brief historical sketch of this "sacred fund," drawn from the laws of Congress and of the State, will establish all I have said.

The s hool fund of Tennessee is, or rather *was*, (for it has ceased to exist since the Bank of Tennessee was invested in Confederate bonds) almost entirely the bounty of the Federal Government. In the year 1796, when the United States ce led to the new State of Tennessee a vast amount of public lands within her borders, it set apart two hundred thousand acres of said land for the benefit of common schools, the proceeds of which, by the express provisions of an act of Congress was to remain *a perpetual fund inviolably for the sup-*

www.ingramcontent.com/pod-product-compliance
Lightning Source LLC
LaVergne TN
LVHW010833120826
845149LV00016B/1354
* 9 7 8 1 4 1 8 1 9 0 4 8 4 *